Rosa Parks

A Little Golden Book® Biography

By Shasta Clinch
Illustrated by Lynn Gaines

 A GOLDEN BOOK • NEW YORK

Golden Books
An imprint of Random House Children's Books • A division of Penguin Random House LLC
1745 Broadway, New York, NY 10019 • penguinrandomhouse.com • rhcbooks.com
Text copyright © 2025 by Shasta Clinch
Cover art and interior illustrations copyright © 2025 by Lynn Gaines
Golden Books, A Golden Book, A Little Golden Book, the G colophon, and the distinctive gold
spine are registered trademarks of Penguin Random House LLC.
Library of Congress Control Number: 2024950027
ISBN 978-0-593-90444-2 (trade) — ISBN 978-0-593-90445-9 (ebook)
Manufactured in the United States of America
10 9 8 7 6 5 4 3 2 1
The authorized representative in the EU for product safety and compliance is Penguin Random
House Ireland, Morrison Chambers, 32 Nassau Street, Dublin D02 YH68, Ireland,
https://eu-contact.penguin.ie.

Rosa Parks was born Rosa Louise McCauley in Tuskegee, Alabama, on February 4, 1913. Her mother was a teacher, and her father was a carpenter. When Rosa was two years old, her parents separated. She moved with her mother and little brother, Sylvester, to live on her grandparents' farm in Pine Level, Alabama.

Rosa's life on the farm was filled with love. But it was hard, too. Every day, she had chores to do. When the chickens laid eggs, she would go to the store with her grandfather to trade them for goods they needed. Her mother taught her how to read and write. She learned how to cook and sew from her grandmother.

Rosa's grandparents were born enslaved. They had been owned by another person and forced to work in terrible conditions without pay. They were freed at the end of the Civil War.

Her mother and grandparents were proud to be Black. They taught Rosa to respect herself and to demand respect from others.

Racial segregation is when people are separated based on the color of their skin. When Rosa was a child, segregation was the law in Alabama and much of the southern United States. Black people had to go to separate schools, eat in separate restaurants, and use separate bathrooms from white people.

COUNTY SCHOOL

Everything was supposed to be separate but equal—but this wasn't true. Schools for white children were clean. They had new schoolbooks and desks for every child. The students were taught through high school.

Rosa's school was a one-room shack with no windows. Black students of different ages learned side by side from old books the white schools threw away. Most schools stopped teaching Black children after sixth grade.

Every day, as Rosa walked to school, she saw a school bus full of white children pass her by. This was one of the first ways Rosa learned about segregation.

Rosa was often sick as a child. She spent a lot of time at home, reading about important Black people in history. She learned about Booker T. Washington, an educator who opened a school for formerly enslaved people, and George Washington Carver, a scientist and inventor.

Booker T. Washington

George Washington Carver

Since Rosa's public school ended after sixth grade, her mother sent her to Montgomery, Alabama, so she could continue her education at a private school. Rosa lived with her aunt and helped pay for her tuition by cleaning and sweeping classrooms. She dreamed of being a nurse or social worker.

But when Rosa was in eleventh grade,
both her grandmother and mother fell ill.
She had to leave school to take care of them.

Rosa met Raymond Parks when she was nineteen. Raymond was a barber. He was also an activist— someone who fights for change. He was a member of the National Association for the Advancement of Colored People (NAACP) and helped the group fight for equal rights for Black people.

Rosa admired Raymond for how he stood up for himself and others. On December 18, 1932, they got married and settled in Montgomery.

Raymond encouraged Rosa to go back to school, and in 1934, she received her high school diploma. She was one of the few Black people in Alabama at that time to finish high school.

Rosa tried to find a job that used her education, but many people still wouldn't hire her because of the color of her skin. She had to take jobs that didn't require a high school diploma, like a cleaner or seamstress.

Her jobs kept her busy, but Rosa couldn't ignore the unfair treatment of Black people in her community. She wanted to do something to help. In 1943, Rosa joined the NAACP, too.

Rosa worked with teenagers in the
NAACP youth programs. She also traveled
around Alabama to listen to the stories of
Black people and the problems they faced.

One of Rosa's biggest projects for the NAACP was helping Black people in Alabama register to vote. Although Black people were allowed to vote, laws in the South made it difficult for them to do so. Some districts required them to own property. Others made them take a test.

Rosa helped inform Black people of their rights and arranged for large groups of Black people to register.

On Thursday, December 1, 1955, Rosa boarded a bus after a long day at work. She sat in the section reserved for Black people. When the bus got crowded, the driver ordered the Black passengers to move to the back of the bus so a white rider could sit down. But Rosa refused to move.

The bus driver got angry. Still, Rosa stayed in her seat. She remembered what her mother and grandparents had taught her about self-respect. She thought of all the hard work she had done with the NAACP. Rosa was tired of giving in to the unfair laws that prevented Black people from having the same rights as white people.

The bus driver called the police. Rosa was arrested and taken to prison. She was released later that night and ordered to pay a fine.

News of Rosa's arrest spread throughout Montgomery. The community came out to support her. They were tired of the unfair laws, too. They decided to stage a bus boycott. Until the law was changed, no Black person in Montgomery, Alabama, would ride on a public bus.

The bus boycott began on December 5, 1955. Instead of riding the bus to work or school, about 40,000 people walked, rode in cabs driven by Black people, or carpooled. As the boycott went on, the bus company started losing a lot of money.

Finally, on November 13, 1956, the Supreme Court ruled that segregated buses were unconstitutional. That means the law went against what was written in the Constitution and had to be changed.

The Montgomery bus boycott ended the following month. It lasted for 381 days—longer than a year! The boycott was one of the biggest and most influential fights against segregation in United States history.

For her role in the bus boycott, Rosa Parks became known as "the mother of the civil rights movement." In 1957, Rosa left Montgomery and moved to Detroit, Michigan, where she continued fighting for equal rights. She attended marches and gave speeches about discrimination.

Rosa Parks received the Presidential Medal of Freedom and the Congressional Gold Medal from President Bill Clinton. *Time* magazine named her one of the most influential people of the twentieth century.

The President of the United States of America

Presidential Medal of Freedon

Rosa L. Parks

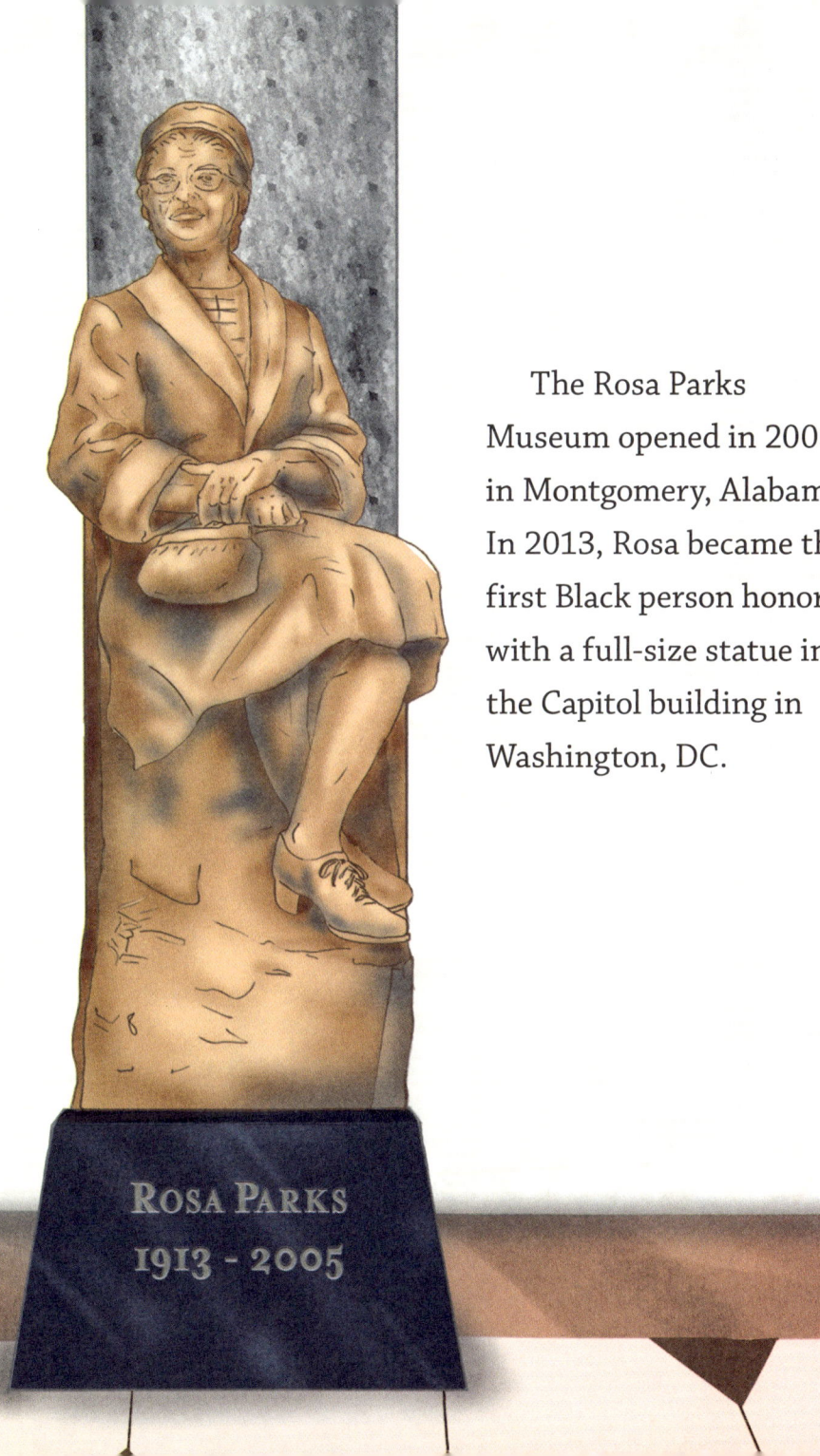

ROSA PARKS
1913 - 2005

The Rosa Parks Museum opened in 2000 in Montgomery, Alabama. In 2013, Rosa became the first Black person honored with a full-size statue in the Capitol building in Washington, DC.

Rosa Parks died on October 24, 2005. She was laid in honor in the Capitol. That is when a private citizen's casket is displayed so people can visit them before they are buried. She was the first woman and second Black person to receive that honor. More than 40,000 people came to say goodbye.

Rosa Parks proved that a small demand for freedom can inspire others and change the world.

"I would like to be remembered as a person who wanted to be free . . . so other people would be also free."